Tring

in old picture postcards volume 2

by
Mike Bass
and
Jill Fowler

European Library – Zaltbommel/Netherlands

Cover picture:
Tring High Street in the 1920s.

The authors:
Jill Fowler and Mike Bass, though not born in Tring, have lived there for most of their lives. Employed in photography for over thirty years, in Akeman Street, one of the oldest parts of the town, they have developed a keen interest in the history of Tring, and particularly the businesses and the people involved in them. Jill has been married to a Tring man for thirty-seven years and her husband's grandfather worked for Lord Rothschild.

GB ISBN 90 288 5639 0 / CIP

© 1993 European Library – Zaltbommel/Netherlands

INTRODUCTION

Welcome to Tring. Much has already been written about the early history of the town and how the four manors of Tring, Miswell, Dunsley and Pendley are mentioned in the Domesday Book, compiled on the instruction of William the Conqueror in 1086. A settlement grew up on an ideal place for trade, where the ancient Icknield Way crossed the Roman road, Akeman Street. It remained a village for many centuries, but with the coming of the Grand Junction canal and the London to Birmingham Railway Company, trade and prosperity increased and started the growth of Tring as a thriving market town.

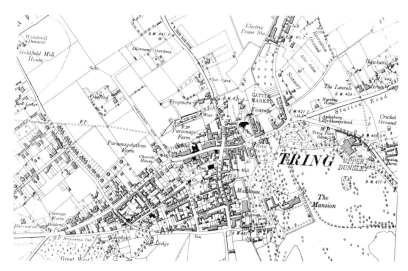

By the end of the 19th century, as well as the larger shops that lined the High Street, there were more than fifty small shops and businesses in the lesser roads on either side of the main route. George Sallery had a butcher's shop, first in Akeman Street and then in the High Street, and continued for many years; older people still remember buying their meat from Sallery's. William Jesse Rodwell was a brewer and soft drinks' manufacturer in Akeman Street and Rodwells is still a thriving business there, more then a hundred years later. There were numerous bootmakers,

tailors and dressmakers and Miss Bethia Horn had a drapery business at 25 Charles Street until well into the 20th century. There was a photographer, Samuel Payne, of Aylesbury, who had a studio in Albert Street and examples of his work still exist.

One of the most significant factors in the shaping of Tring was the coming of the Rothschild family. Lionel Rothschild purchased Tring Park in 1837, with the mansion, which was later encased and extended by Nathaniel, first Lord Rothschild. The mansion is now occupied by The Arts Educational School. The Rothschilds provided work and trade for much of Tring's population, especially when the museum was built to house Walter Rothschild's collection of insects, birds and animals, the building starting in 1889. It is now part of the British Museum and attracts thousands of people a year to its public displays, which are especially popular with children. G. Grace & Son, still a family hardware business in the High Street, have records of purchases by the Rothschilds, including fitting exhibition cases for the displays and designing the central heating system. James Honour had a builder's yard in Akeman Street, where highly skilled staff manufactured all that was needed to build to Rothschild requirements. Now a collection of small businesses occupy the site, still known locally as 'Honours Yard'. Lord Rothschild was also the host to the nobility and photographs show that Tring welcomed the Prince of Wales, later King Edward VII, on several occasions.

One of Tring's greatest assets is the beautiful countryside that surrounds it, much of it crossed by footpaths and available to the public. There are some of the best beech woods in the Chilterns at Ashridge, now owned by the National Trust, and the chalk downlands produce a wide variety of wild flowers.

At the beginning of the 20th century the Tring area was recorded as containing 3,120 acres of arable land, 3,310 acres of permanent grass and 815 acres of woodland. A large number of the inhabitants were occupied in agriculture and sheep farming.

Now let us begin our journey back in time to see Tring as it used to be. Starting at the West End of the town, where the road comes in from Aylesbury, we will go straight through to the London road, pointing out places of interest on the way. We will then explore the side roads and finally take you along Station Road to Tring Station, where you should be able to get a train to London at the end of your day.

We have tried to show you photographs that include parts of modern day Tring, to ensure that you do not lose your way, but where buildings or whole areas have been demolished this has not always been possible. We hope you enjoy your visit to old Tring.

Acknowledgements:
We would like to thank Mrs. Peggy Slemeck and Mr. John Rotheroe for letting us copy some of their old postcards; also the Hertfordshire County Record Office for allowing us to use the two Buckler prints (volume 1) of Tring Church. We are especially grateful to Mr. Bob Grace, not only for the use of some of the photographs from his collection, and his advice, but also for the generous help he has given over the years to all of us who are keen to learn more about old Tring.

1. On arriving in Tring we find on our right, on the corner of Duckmore Lane, The Bricklayers Arms, photographed about 1870. Behind the yew trees are a row of cottages known as Bottle Cross and Hobbs stonemeason's yard. Twenty years later 36 year-old George Wright was the publican, a bricklayer by trade, with his wife Mary Ann and their four children. There is no sign of any of these buildings remaining now, though the Britannia seen here in the background has altered little.

Western Road, Tring.

S. G. Payne & Son, Aylesbury.

2. The Britannia public house in about 1910, looking much as it does today. It was built by John Brown, of Tring Brewery, in the 1840s, chiefly to cater for the navvies working on the London to Birmingham Railway. The motor works Wright & Wright are behind the houses on the left. They were established in 1870 by Mr. George Parrott, who took Mr. A.S. Wright into partnership in 1901. Mr. Wright succeeded to the business and in 1911 took his cousin, Mr. R.G. Wright, as his partner. The business, with larger premises now fronting the road, is still there today.

WESTERN RD. TRING

3. We now go further along Western Road, approaching the town centre as it was in about 1916. Most of the buildings shown here have altered little in nearly eighty years. The tobacconist's shop is still a newsagents and tobacconists but printing, bookbinding and hair cutting are no longer carried on there. The shop beyond was that of Mr. George Thorpe, the grocer. The tall houses on the right are still private dwellings, and the high roof of the Baptist Church can be seen beyond.

4. Ivy Cottage on the Western Road in about 1880. It was known as a dame school, where children were taught the skills of straw plaiting, and was run by Miss Wilson. The wooden building beyond was the workshop of the Pusey family, who were the estate carpenters to Pendley. The National School can just be seen on the left and the school house was behind it. Ivy cottage was later demolished and replaced by shops, the Library stands on the site of the National School.

High Street, Tring.

5. The other side of Western Road about 1910, which is now the High Street, viewed looking down from the previous photograph. The Tring Gazette then had its office in the town; next door Cosier & Son were high-class tailors. A little further down, the furniture shop, Brandon's, was a thriving business until quite recently.

6. Looking down the High Street in the late 1890s with Ivy Cottage still on the left and the Post Office on the right. At this time Mr. William Rodwell was postmaster. Letters arrived from all parts at 4 a.m. and deliveries were at 7 and 9 a.m. and at 4 and 6 p.m.

7. One last look back the way we have come, the Post Office is on the left and Mr. Foskett can just be seen in the doorway of his boot and shoe shop. On the right Mr. Hedges had his painter's and decorator's shop. Beyond that is G. Grace and Sons hardware shop, established in the 18th century. The 1891 census reveals Mr. Gilbert Grace there with his wife Emma and four children, the oldest being nine year-old Gilbert, grandfather of the present Mr. Gilbert Grace.

8. The architect's drawing of the new Market House by Mr. William Huckvale, Lord Rothschild's architect, responsible for many other buildings in Tring including the picturesque Louisa Cottages in Park Road. The local paper at the time says 'it was erected by the inhabitants of Tring as a Memorial to her Majesty's Diamond Jubilee. The cost of the building and site was £2,400 and all the money, we believe, is now raised'. It was opened in 1901.

9. The crossroads showing Akeman Street to the right and Frogmore Street to the left, in the mid-1890s. The building on the left was soon to be demolished, to make room for the extended George public house. Just beyond on the left was the old Post Office, soon to be replaced with a shop of a more elaborate design. Many of the buildings further down the High Street you will still be able to recognise.

10. The Old George public house in Frogmore Street near the corner with Western Road, now the High Street, in about 1897. It was described as a small hostelry and corn chandlers' store held in 1806 by Mr. Joseph Tompkins and by Mr. William Clarke in 1830. It was rebuilt and enlarged to reach the High Street at the end of the 19th century, by the Aylesbury Brewery Company.

11. Sheep in the High Street about the turn of the century. On the left is Manchester House, Greenings the outfitters. In later years Mr. Raymond Herman was a popular figure selling gentlemen's clothes. Mr. Jack Clement, the jeweller next door, continued his business there for another half century. Tring Brewery is on the right.

High Street, Tring.

12. The High Street, looking back, about 1914. On the left are Westwood & Dellar, green-grocer; Thomas Glover, grocer; the National Provincial Bank, John Bly Antiques and Tring Brewery, the large entranceway in the centre. It was owned by John Brown from the 1830s until he sold it to Lock and Smith of Berkhamsted in 1898. On the right the Bell Inn, one of the oldest surviving public houses in Tring. We are told that 'in 1611 Henry Geary was before the Justices for keeping the Bell without a licence and a few years later for drunkenness'.

13. We turn round again and continue our journey through Tring to see the Old Rose and Crown in about 1895. It was an old coaching inn and in those days was level with the other buildings. The three-gabled building, just before the entrance to Tring Park, is much the same today. It had been re-fronted in the style approved by the Rothschilds.

14. An early photograph of the High Street. The large building just seen on the left is now Brown & Merry's, the estate agent. The next row of shops, now gone, were Mr. Grace's hardware shop, Mr. Thorpe's, wholesale grocers; and Mr. Johnson, the fishmonger. Then we can just see the old Market House. It must have been a hot day, as the shops have their blinds down and the big upper doors of the Market House are open.

15. The Market House obscured the view of the church that we now enjoy, seen here about 1900. Records state that there was a Market House in Tring in 1650 with a corn loft over it. In 1819 it was described as 'a mean edifice on wooden pillars having a pillory and cage underneath'. It was demolished in 1900.

High Street, Tring.

16. We are now approaching the far end of Tring High Street in about 1895. The well-known Fulks family are still involved in business in the town. The Plough Hotel, later a shop, was for many years the premises of John Bly Antiques. The shop beyond, now Metcalfes, was that of Mr. Tompkins, ironmonger and pastrycook. The newspaper office on the far right was replaced in 1897 by the mock timbered dwelling now called 'Oasis'. It was built for the Rothschild Estate Accountant.

17. The Green Man Inn, Lower High Street. John Philby brewed here in 1846 and John Woodman from 1878 to 1895. It was pulled down by the Rothschilds about 1895. Mr. Woodman is standing in the doorway and Mr. Knight is on the left of the group. Another well-known family, the Gowers, had the shop in centre on the left-hand side.

18. At the end of the last century there were two Co-operative stores in Tring; the one shown here at the far end of the town was built in about 1880, the one in Charles Street we will visit later. Both continued to trade until well into the next century. The High Street branch is now the Frances Elizabeth Crystal Rooms, used for wedding receptions and other events.

19. We have now reached the point where the High Street continues, to become the London Road, the turning to the right being Brook Street. The wall on the left shows where Lower Dunsley was situated, but in this photograph, taken about 1906, the village had gone and Lord Rothschild's water garden had taken its place. It is now the Memorial Garden. Roberts and Wilsons Robin Hood is on the right. It was a 17th century building, but much restored and altered and in 1806 it was kept by William Tapping.

20. This picture of Brook End taken about 1880, shows Lower Dunsley on the left, with the Green Man in the distance. Records tell us that 'Dunsley was annexed to Pendley in the 15th century but later formed part of the Tring Park Estate and was called Upper Dunsley'. The Robin Hood is in the centre.

21. Lower Dunsley about 1870, viewed from the Robin Hood Corner. It was quite a thriving community in those days, the Burgess brothers' weaving shop on the left and the Manor Brewery on the right. The Manor Brewery, sited at 172 High Street, Lower Dunsley, brewed from 1839 to 1895 and was run by the Liddingtons.

22. Now let's turn back to explore the side streets of Tring, but on our way we must find out something about Tring Park and the Mansion. These elegant gates, made by Mr. Gilbert Grace, are decorated with The Prince of Wales' feathers, made from flowers, for Prince Edward's visit. Sadly the gates went for scrap during the Second World War. This is now the entrance to Mansion Drive, a small collection of modern detached homes. The buildings on either side are unaltered and still in use.

23. Tring Mansion as it used to be. It was built by Henry Guy, Groom of the Bedchamber to King Charles II, and is attributed to Christopher Wren. The Tring Estate was sold to Baron Lionel Nathan de Rothschild in 1873. Mr. William Kay, the previous owner, died in 1865.

TRING PARK

24. Tring Park and Mansion, showing emus and rheas in the foreground. The old building was enclosed by the Rothschilds to look as it does today, and the left-hand top wing was added in about 1898. The flag is the Royal Standard for visiting royalty. Baron Lionel de Rothschild was succeeded in 1879 by Mr. Nathan Mayer de Rothschild, who was created Lord Rothschild of Tring.

25. Lord Walter Rothschild and his zebra cart. The zebras had their feet cared for by the local blacksmith, Mr. Eric Reed. The smithy in the High Street is now a doctor's surgery.

26. A much older Lord Walter Rothschild presenting a book and a small token to the children of Tring to celebrate the Silver Jubilee of King George V. The recipient is Donald Reed, son of the blacksmith. Young Donald later became a well-known photographer in the town and although he has now retired, there are still three shops in the area that bear his name.

27. The park was the venue of the Annual Tring Show, the largest one-day show in the country. There were classes for all types of farm animals as well as dog trials and show jumping. Lord Rothschild was particularly interested in breeding heavy horses and had a stud farm just outside Tring. Young Miss Rodwell stands at the front of this photograph taken by her father, William J. Rodwell.

28. As we went through the gates of Tring Park, we saw that they were decorated to welcome a visit from the Prince of Wales. Now, as we return to the High Street and turn left towards the crossroads, we find that the town is also decorated to celebrate the occasion. The familiar tile-hung building on the left remains today. The old Rose and Crown is next to it, with staff in the doorway, no doubt hoping to see the prince arrive.

Rose & Crown Hotel. Tring.

29. Retracing our steps back to the town centre perhaps we will pause for refreshment at the new Rose and Crown, rebuilt by the Rothschild Estate 1905-1906. This picture, taken from the church tower, shows the park and mansion in the background. The hotel was passed to the Hertfordshire Public House Trust, now Trust House Forte. It is still a delightful place to call into for a drink or a meal.

High Street, Tring.

S. G. Payne & Son, Aylesbury.

30. We have now reached the crossroads again and it is about 1904. The Market House has been built. It was enclosed in 1910. Part of the George Hotel can be seen on the right. We will now turn left into Akeman Street.

31. Early in the century army manoeuvres were held annually and public houses had to keep their stables available. The soldiers and their mounts gather in Akeman Street by the side of the Market House. Stables can be seen in the background.

Akeman Street, Tring.

S. G. Payne & Son, Aylesbury.

32. The Victoria Works in Akeman Street in about 1910. A directory of 1890 said that the Victoria Hall was erected in 1886 on the site of the former assembly room built in 1825. It was designed by Mr. William Huckvale, architect of Tring. It was later changed to the Victoria Works and produced mineral water, cider, pickles and vinegar. It resumed its former name and housed the Tring Library for many years and is now used for meetings and exhibitions as before.

33. Further along Akeman Street about 1900. On the left the entrance to Clement Place led to a yard surrounded by cottages, in one of which lived Mrs. Massey, mother of the Victorian poet and mystic Gerald Massey. The white building beyond is the front of Mr. Thomas Grace's yard. Mr. Grace is in the centre on his tricycle. He was the maltster and corn and seed merchant. The area, although now considerably altered, is still called Grace's Maltings. On the right is The Harrow public house. Beyond this, on the same side, can be seen the hotel called the Temperance Hotel, kept by Mr. Joseph Piggott at the turn of the century and later by Mrs. Ellen Piggott.

Akeman St., Tring

34. The Harrow public house in Akeman Street. The publican in 1890 was Miss Ann Miller and after her, until 1917, came Mr. William Fleet, Mr. George Woodward, Mr. Willis Horn and Mr. Henry Watson. In this photograph it was unoccupied and was pulled down shortly afterwards.

35. The Grace family in the garden of Grace's Maltings in about 1880. It was a malting in medieval times and continued to be used as one until after the First World War. It continued as a corn mill for about another fifty years, chiefly in the care of Mr. Bob Grace, still a popular local figure. He is well-known for his 'Old Tring' lantern lectures and for his fund of knowledge about the history of the town and its people. His father, Mr. Frank Grace, an enthusiastic photographer, took many of the early photographs of Tring.

36. We have now reached the far end of Akeman Street and are looking back. On the left is the Jolly Sportsman public house. In 1891 the publican was 57 year-old Mr. Jesse Thorn, who lived there with his wife Mary Ann. A few doors down was the Swan public house, with 64 year-old Joseph Gurney and his wife, also named Mary Ann. The Old Swan, now a private house, is now the last building on that side, the others being demolished to build the Louisa Cottages. On the right is the entrance to Town Farm.

37. Just round the corner, turning left into Park Street, we find the earliest part of the Natural History Museum. It was a gabled, tile-hung building, dating from 1889. It was built by Lord Rothschild to house young Walter's collection and library and to provide a cottage for Mr. Alfred Minall, the taxidermist. Park Street was originally called Maidenhead Street.

38. With our backs to Park Street we are looking up Park Road about the turn of the century. On our right is the first group of the almshouses, Louisa Cottages, built in 1893 and extended in 1901. They were originally built to house retired workers from the Rothschild estate.

39. In Park Road looking back towards the museum, at the turn of the century. The large houses on the left have remained almost the same to this day. The track to the right is one entrance to Prospect House School.

40. Prospect House School from The Castle public house, showing the inn's railings in the foreground and the brick wall the other side of Langdon Street. One of the first headmasters of the school was Dr. Clarabut, the New Mill pastor, later Mr. Mark Young, and by 1899 Mr. Charles William Maull was the assistant head teacher. When Prospect House was demolished he took the school to Brookfield, New Mill. The wall on the left marks the boundary of the villa 'Belle Vue', for some time the home of Dr. and Mrs. Knox.

41. Further along Park Road in about 1910, showing the Tring Station Omnibus. These houses remain today, looking much the same. In the distance is The Castle public house, the publican being Mr. George Robert Ives.

42. Continuing along Park Road we come to Cato's canvas weaving shop. Cato's started originally in Tabernacle Yard, Akeman Street and George Cato went to 12 Charles Street, where as early as 1871 there had been a canvas weaver named Mr. Henry Higgs. This photograph was taken in the Park Road premises, now no longer there. On the left is Mr. Ward, Mr. Cato is the man on the right with the beard. The boys were 'half-timers' from school.

43. At the junction just beyond Cato's we look right, down Chapel Street, and see Harry Fincher's general stores in 1917. Mrs. Fincher is standing in the doorway with her Saturday help, Miss Simmonds. No shops remain in Chapel Street today. Fincher's also had a shop in the High Street, now a wool shop, and Mrs. Fincher was famous for her delicious turkish delight, made in Watford.

44. Between Park Road and Chapel Street, King Street turns back in the direction of the town centre. In King Street, once called Pleasant Lane, we see a German touring band in the street. In the background we just can see The King's Arms, built by John Brown in the 1830s. From records of 1891 we see 64 year-old Mr. Joseph Lewis from Marsworth was then the landlord, with his wife, Jane. This photograph was taken in about 1910, when Mr. Charles Murphy was the landlord.

45. Approaching the King's Arms we turn right and come into Charles Street. Just round the corner is Howlett's Stores. In the 1880s it was Mr. Ernest Wright's furniture shop, but had changed to the hardware shop by 1917, which it remained for many years. Mr. Howlett was a familiar figure doing a round selling paraffin, first with a pony and cart and later with a van. Mr. Howlett's brother, Cyril, who had a Post Office and general store in King Street, was a keen photographer and took several of the postcards featured here. In this photograph we see young Margaret Howlett and her brother Leonard, holding their dog Peter.

46. At the other end of the road was the Tring Co-operative Grocery and Provisions Stores at No. 1 Charles Street. The photograph was taken in October 1906, showing the manager and his staff. It was a busy shop until fairly recently, but has now been converted into several homes.

47. We will now cross to the other side of the main road, to where Miswell Lane turns off to join the Icknield Way. On the left-hand side we find Mr. Robert Hedges stores, the shop still a busy general store called The Old Stables. This photograph shows the Tring fire brigade posing in front of the shop which was originally built as a veterinary surgery for Mr. Seeley Green.

Miswell Lane, Tring.

S. G. Payne & Son, Aylesbury.

48. Continuing up Miswell Lane in about 1910. Opposite these houses were open fields looking across to Oakford, where later the Osmington School for boys was built. Miswell Lane was also sometimes called Windmill Lane.

MISWELL LANE. TRING

49. Looking back down Miswell Lane with the downs and woodlands in the background. The houses on the left were built to rehouse people in Tring, including the straw plaiters in Harrow Yard, when their old cottages were demolished.

50. An early photograph of the Icknield Way, facing east, with Miswell Lane and the Gold-field Mill to the right. The mill was built in 1840 by Mr. Grover. Formerly in partnership with the Mead family, who had their business at New Mill, Mr. Grover had a disagreement with Mr. Mead, so he built his own mill by the Icknield Way.

51. The Lodge at Dundale built by the Rothschilds, from a William Huckvale design, as a luncheon hut for their fishing parties. It was also used by their guests, shooting partridge in the local fields. It is now in ruins.

52. 'Uncle' Street in a punt on the lake at Dundale. He often complained that the local cats caught the fish, which were the indigenous brown trout, said to be far superior in taste to the rainbow trout.

53. Rheas, ostrich and young peacocks being fed at Dundale by Lord Rothschild's keeper 'Uncle' Street, who was in charge of the trout lake and the birds.

54. Leaving Dundale on our left we continue down Dundale Road towards the town centre, where it becomes Frogmore Street. On the high bank on the right was Bunstrux manor house, approached by a flight of stone steps. An Inventory of the Historical Monuments of Hertfordshire in 1910 described it as 'apparently 16th century, now uninhabited, walls of brick and timber. Condition: Very dilapidated, the timbers are decaying and the plaster is falling off'. Other records describe Mr. Harcourt, then Lord of the Manor in the early part of the 19th century, sitting at the top of the steps collecting his dues. It was later two cottages and has now been demolished.

55. Further down Frogmore Street, Alma Place, also known as Big Place, in about 1900. It consisted of these cottages in the front and others surrounding a yard behind, the whole area listing 44 people in the 1891 Census. Westwood Lane leads up to the church on the right. It is now a car park and Barnetts the bakers is just on the left-hand side.

56. With our backs to the town crossroads we are looking back down Frogmore Street about 1890. On the left is the Manse for the New Mill Chapel. The house with the railings was later Johnson's wet fish shop and is now Foxy's restaurant. In the far distance is Barnets the bakers. Just beyond the lamp-post is the Dolphin Inn. Tring charity records state that 'three tenements in Church Lane, lately known as the Dolphin Beer House have recently been sold to the Reverend Arthur Frederick Pope and by him converted into a Workman's Hall'. It is now part of the area known as Dolphin Square, Tring's shopping precinct.

57. A short cut up Church Lane takes us to have a look at Tring Church. This photograph shows the back of the old cottages in Church Lane. Beyond is the Vestry Hall, still there, the only part of this area not demolished. The Vestry Cottages were charity cottages, let at one shilling a week.

58. The Vestry Hall when it housed the fire engine. It was a civic building, built about 1866, and was also a police station. The fire engine, which was pulled by horses, did about two-hundred years service, until the 1930s. Many of the crew were employees of Mr. Gilbert Grace, who was the captain, though not in this picture. Fourth from the right is Mr. John Bly, grandfather of the present John Bly, well-known in the antiques business and on television.

59. The West view of Tring Church showing cottages in Westwood Lane, now no longer there. The lane did not reach the west door, but turned to the right some yards from the church. This is the entrance through which the bride will enter with her father to start the wedding ceremony.

Tring Church.

60. St. Peter and St. Paul's Church, showing the south side, little altered since this photograph was taken in about 1910, though the railings have now gone. The church contains six bells, dating from 1624 to 1882. The interior was thoroughly restored in 1862, and was partially rebuilt in the early 1880s. The restoration, which was completed in March 1882, cost about £3,500, raised by voluntary contributions. The register dates from 1566. The archway to the right gave entry to the Vicarage.

61. The other side of the archway showing the north side of Tring Church behind. The old Vicarage is now part of Sutton Court, the premises of the Sutton Housing Trust.

Brook Street, Tring.

62. Going back towards the London end of Tring we turn left down Brook Street again seeing the Robin Hood and beyond it Mr. W. Bly's shop. At one time there used to be stocks in the centre for the wrongdoers of Wigginton. Wigginton Manor is on the right.

63. A little further down Brook Street we now find the Tring Market. This was built by the Rothschilds at the turn of the century; earlier it would have been held in the High Street, 'Market Street'. There has been a livestock market since the 13th century. A market is held on Fridays, according to a charter of Charles II, who decreed that straw plait should be sold in the morning and the corn after mid-day. The corn trade was later done on Fridays at the Market House.

64. Looking up the Feeder in Brook Street about 1913, with the gas works in the background. The trees were being cleared as the Rothschilds were going to build cottages here, but the plan was abandoned when the ground was found to be too waterlogged.

NEW MILL, TRING, HERTS.

Photo., Copyright J. T NEWMAN BERKHAMPSTED

65. New Mill in about 1900. The houses on the right, known as Eighteen Row, were pulled down and replaced by cottages.

66. Tring dockyard and boat building yard, New Mill, Tring, with the Tring Flour Mills in the background. The dockyard was owned by W. Mead and Co. and was taken over by Bushell Bros. in March 1912.

67. Left: The mill, used by Meads Flour Mills, by the canal at New Mill, Tring. It was earlier Mr. Grover's mill. Right: It was knocked down in the 1930s. The man on the right is Mr. George Hall, who worked for Bushell Bros. Mr. Hall later had his own business in Western Road, as a blacksmith, with much of his work consisting of making the metal rims for cart wheels. His workshop is now part of the Tring Service Station.

68. The workers photographed by the mill when it was being demolished.

69. Since Tring, in the early part of the century, was largely an agricultural town, we will take a quick look at the farming community. Mr. Philby, from Mew Mill, is operating his steam engine driving the threshing machine. This photograph, taken in Hountslow Field, shows the children, sitting on four bushel sacks, on an August bank holiday. Houses in Longfield Road can be seen in the background.

70. Threshing at Miswell Farm. On the left is Mr. Tom Grace, then Mr. George Bradding and Mr. 'Higby' Knock.

71. Rabbits caught in the harvest fields at Miswell Farm. There are members of several Tring families here, including the Jakemans, Kempsters, Hearns and Wilkins. The gentleman with the gun is Mr. Bob Grace. The rabbits made a welcome addition to the diets of local people.

72. Now we must make our way down Station Road, but will stop a moment to look at Pendley Manor on the right-hand side of the road. The original Pendley Manor is mentioned in the Domesday Book. It was confiscated by William the Conqueror in 1066 and had a succession of owners, until it was abandoned at the beginning of the 19th century by Sir Simon Harcourt, who objected to the disturbance caused by the construction of the nearby canal and railway. It burned down in 1835 and was rebuilt by Joseph Grout Williams J.P. later in the century. It is now a hotel and conference centre.

73. The route to the station is still a pleasant road lined by old chestnut trees and farmland. Before the parapet was heightened, the bridge was the site of a tragic accident. Mr. and Mrs. Knight were driving home in their trap when the pony was frightened by a train and bolted. As the cart swung over the bridge the couple were thrown out and toppled over the low parapet. Mr. Knight was killed, but Mrs. Knight survived and lived to be ninety. Their daughter, Miss Knight, who used to teach in the Sunday School, was a well-known figure and lived in Akeman Street until she was over a hundred. The penny stamp shows King Edward VII, who was a welcome visitor to Tring. He succeeded his mother, Queen Victoria, to the throne in 1901.

74. We are now almost at the end of our journey as we approach Tring Station. The drawing shows the Tring cutting in the course of construction by the London and Birmingham Railway Company. It followed almost the same route as the canal, constructed earlier, but had to be deeper, hence the system of ramps and pulleys to remove soil, devised by James Stephenson. The Tring cutting was 2¼ miles long and 57 feet deep. The West Herts Hospital had 43 admissions arising from accidents during the work, six of which were fatal.

75. A meet of hounds in the forecourt of Tring Station. The station masters house can be seen on the right-hand side, later demolished. This photograph was probably taken from a window in the Royal Hotel, one of John Brown's many public houses, formerly called The Harcourt Arms.

76. Tring Station. In 1890 it was described as 'a London and North Western Railway Station, 31³/₄ miles from London and 1³/₄ miles from Tring'. Since electrification in 1966 it is possible to get to London in less than an hour. Thank you for coming on this nostalgic look at old Tring. We hope you have enjoyed it.